ideals special issue

The Spirit of America

A nation is its people, and its energy and spirit.

These are gifts given in abundance to America.

Nowhere has history recorded the presence of so much promise and opportunity. Go ahead and criticize your country if you wish. That is the secret of our success. But when you do, remember that your right to speak freely is a rare and precious privilege in a world of tyranny.

Feel proud of your country for you have every right to admire its accomplishments and its standard of human dignity. We have opened our hearts, our doors and our resources whenever the world called out for help. We have asked nothing in return.

America is the serenity of a Wisconsin dairy farm at sunset; the majesty of the Rockies. It is the hum of New York and the unrestrained joy of New Orleans, the distant honk of low flying geese and the solitary stalk of the cougar.

It is beauty, promise and faith. One cannot ask for more.

William Proxmire
United States Senator

Cover painting by John Slobodnik

THE MEMORY OF ... IS ENSHRINED FOREVER

United We Stand

America

God built Him a continent of glory
   and filled it with treasures untold;
He carpeted it with soft-rolling prairies
   and columned it with thundering mountains;
He studded it with sweet-flowing fountains
   and traced it with long-winding streams;
He planted it with deep-shadowed forests
   and filled them with song.
Then He called unto a thousand peoples
   and summoned the bravest among them.

They came from the ends of the earth,
   each bearing a gift and a hope.
The glow of adventure was in their eyes,
   and in their hearts the glory of hope.

And out of the bounty of earth and the labor of men,
Out of the longing of hearts and the prayer of souls,
Out of the memory of ages and hopes of the world,
God fashioned a nation in love, blessed it with
Purpose sublime ... and called it America!

Abba Hillel Silver

The People

This land whose founders cherished liberty
Produced a people venturesome and strong,
With kindness as untrammeled as the sea,
Keen, homespun humor and contempt for wrong.
Their ax blades rang, their rough-hewn plows cut straight
Across the sod. They sowed their lives like seed
Into the nation they envisioned great,
Resolved to make their dream accomplished deed.

From the four corners of the world they came
To build the new republic which would rise
In startling splendor, like a comet's flame,
Whose sudden brilliance floods the star-strewn skies.
They left a heritage by life and death:
The land where freedom breathed her first pure breath.

Gail Brook Burket

The Concord Hymn

Ralph Waldo Emerson

By the rude bridge that arched the flood,
Their flag to April's breeze unfurled,
Here once the embattled farmers stood,
And fired the shot heard round the world.

The foe long since in silence slept;
Alike the conqueror silent sleeps;
And Time the ruined bridge has swept
Down the dark stream which seaward creeps.

On this green bank, by this soft stream,
We set today a votive stone;
That memory may their deed redeem,
When, like our sires, our sons are gone.

Spirit, that made those spirits dare
To die, and leave their children free,
Bid Time and Nature gently spare
The shaft we raise to them and thee.

Bedford Flag

The Bedford Flag is a mailed arm extending from a cloud, the arm clasping a sword. On the scroll are inscribed the words, "Vince Aut Morire" . . . Conquer or Die.

The three disks represent cannonballs. This is one of the most interesting of the flags. It is one of the first flags of the American Revolution to receive a baptism of British fire. It was carried at Lexington and Concord by the minutemen of Bedford on April 19, 1775.

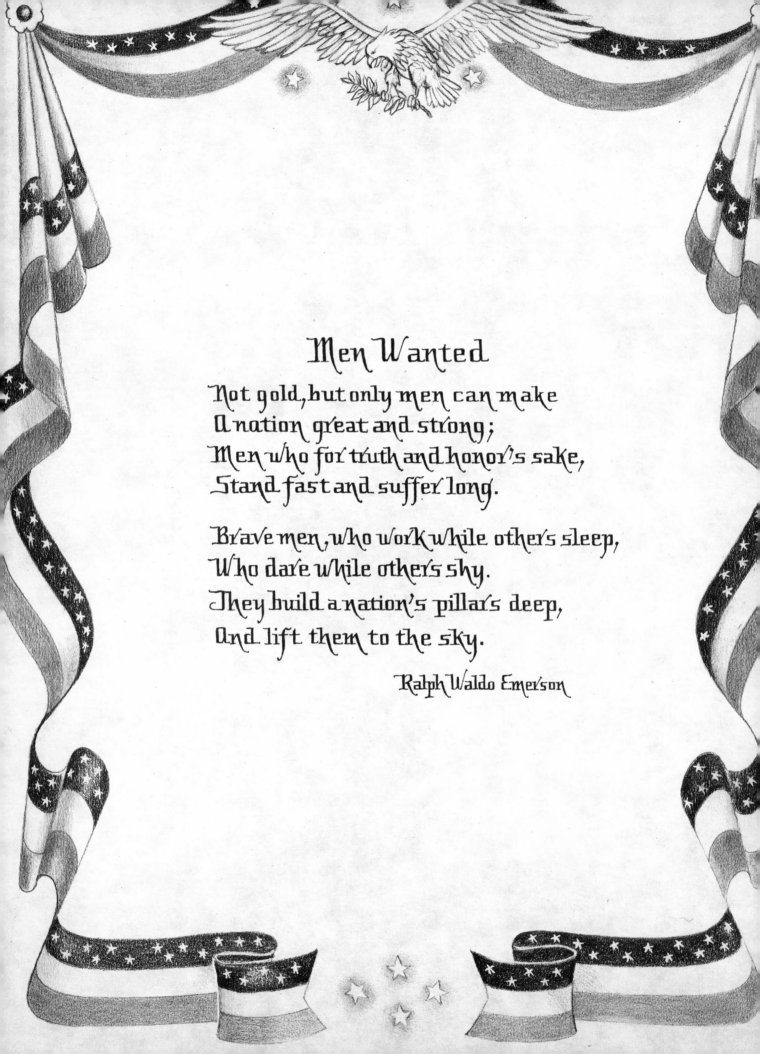

Men Wanted

Not gold, but only men can make
A nation great and strong;
Men who for truth and honor's sake,
Stand fast and suffer long.

Brave men, who work while others sleep,
Who dare while others shy.
They build a nation's pillars deep,
And lift them to the sky.

Ralph Waldo Emerson

First in war, first in peace and
first in the hearts of his countrymen,
he was second to none in the humble and
endearing scenes of private life.

Henry Lee
December 26, 1799

George Washington

From 1752 until 1759 George Washington's military service, as aide to General Braddock and as commander of Virginia militia, permitted only infrequent visits to Mount Vernon. During this period the plantation was managed by his younger brother, John Augustine. Fort Duquesne fell in November, 1758, and George Washington retired to private life. In January, 1759 he married Martha Dandridge Custis, widow of Daniel Parke Custis. To an English friend he wrote, "I am now, I believe, fixed at this Seat with an agreeable Consort for Life and hope to find more happiness in retirement than I ever experienced amidst a wide and bustling World." This expectation of retirement was to be disappointed, but the peaceful years together at Mount Vernon before the Revolution were the happiest of their lives. There is an echo of this in the lines George Washington wrote to his wife from Philadelphia in 1775, on the eve of his departure for New England as newly appointed Commander in Chief of the Continental Army: "I should enjoy more real happiness in one month with you at home than I have the most distant prospect of finding abroad, if my stay were to be seven times seven years."

During the war years Martha Washington spent eight winters with her husband in his northern encampments, from the first at Cambridge to the last at Newburgh, leaving Mount Vernon in the late autumn and returning in the spring as the opening guns announced a new military campaign. George Washington stopped briefly at Mount Vernon en route to and from Yorktown in 1781. Lund Washington, distant cousin and faithful friend, managed the estate in his absence. General Washington resigned his commission at Annapolis in December, 1783, and returned to Mount Vernon. Once again he looked forward to the life of a private citizen and husbandman on the bank of the Potomac, but again he was disappointed. He remained at Mount Vernon until he assumed the Presidency in 1789, but his fame and inevitable position as leader in the movement for a stronger union denied him the domestic ease he desired.

Excerpt from MOUNT VERNON, AN ILLUSTRATED
HANDBOOK, Copyright © 1972 by The Mount
Vernon Ladies' Association of the Union

He paced the knoll to find the perfect site
On which to build a house his very own,
Well-planned to give protection and delight.
Regard for excellence and good taste shone
In lines which seemed inevitably right,
As his house grew from dreams which he had sown.
Sun blessed by day and moon adorned by night,
It soon loomed proudly on its hill alone.

For years this house has stood with ageless grace,
Superb proportions that enchant the eye,
And cornice, chimney, wall and roof which trace
Their frozen melody against the sky.
Those who have seen its beauty have all known
That love and honor were its cornerstone.

Gail Brook Burket

Monticello

High on the top of Little Mountain, near Charlottesville in Albemarle County, Virginia, stands Monticello, home of Thomas Jefferson, begun in 1768, eight years before our War of Independence. It was not completed until the close of his second term as President of the United States. In a letter, dated 1786, Jefferson described the setting: *Where has nature spread so rich a mantle under the eye? Mountains, forests, rocks, rivers. With what majesty do we ride above the storm! How sublime to look down into the workhouse of nature, to see her clouds, hail, snow, rain, thunder, all fabricated at our feet! And the glorious Sun, when rising as if out of a distant water, just gilding the tops of the mountains, and giving life to all nature.*

Jefferson, in laying out Monticello, deviated from the usually accepted plan of a ménage, which included a main or big house and a series of small outbuildings consisting of a kitchen, laundry, smokehouse, dairy, stable, weaving house, and sometimes a schoolhouse. He employed long terraces, with a promenade, which formed a "U" with the mansion, extending from it in opposite directions for some sixty feet, at which point each terrace turned at a right angle and extended to the west, terminating with two balanced out-chambers, the "Honeymoon Cottage" on the south and Colonel Randolph's study in like position on the north. Jefferson was able to place out of view from the house, beneath the terraces, the dependencies such as the kitchen, the cook's room, servants' rooms, dairy, and the room for smoking meat on the south side, and the stables, the carriage house, icehouse and laundry on the north. By means of an all-weather passageway running under the house for its full width, the rooms beneath the north and south terraces were connected one with the other and also with the mansion on the basement level.

An architectural masterpiece, Monticello is one of the best examples of the classical revival style, on which Thomas Jefferson was the first exponent. It is a superlative document, displaying the taste and skill of the first architect of the Republic.

Randle Bond Truett

From MONTICELLO, Copyright © 1957 by Randle Bond Truett, by permission of HASTINGS HOUSE, PUBLISHERS.

Elfreth's Alley: Since 1690 the oldest continuously inhabited street in the United States.

Benjamin Franklin and Philadelphia

From his "Autobiography,"
Benjamin Franklin
describes his first acquaintance
with the "City of Brotherly Love"
as a young man of twenty.

I have been the more particular in this description of my journey, and shall be so of my first entry into that city, that you may in your mind compare such unlikely beginnings with the figure I have since made there. I was in my working dress, my best cloaths being to come round by sea. I was dirty from my journey; my pockets were stuff'd out with shirts and stockings, and I knew no soul nor where to look for lodging. I was fatigued with travelling, rowing and want of rest, I was very hungry; and my whole stock of cash consisted of a Dutch dollar, and about a shilling in copper. The latter I gave the people of the boat for my passage, who at first refus'd it, on account of my rowing; but I insisted on their taking it. A man being sometimes more generous when he has but a little money than when he has plenty, perhaps thro' fear of being thought to have but little.

Then I walked up the street, gazing about till near the market-house I met a boy with bread. I had made many a meal on bread, and, inquiring where he got it, I went immediately to the baker's he directed me to, in Second-street, and ask'd for bisket, intending such as we had in Boston; but they, it seems, were not made in Philadelphia. Then I asked for a three-penny loaf, and was told they had none such. So not considering or knowing the difference of money, and the greater cheapness nor the names of his bread, I bad him give me three-penny worth of any sort. He gave me, accordingly, three great puffy rolls. I was surpriz'd at the quantity, but took it, and, having no room in my pockets, walk'd off with a roll under each arm, and eating the other. Thus I went up Market-street as far as Fourth-street, passing by the door of Mr. Read, my future wife's father; when she, standing at the door, saw me, and thought I made, as I certainly did, a most awkward, ridiculous appearance. Then I turned and went down Chestnut-street and part of Walnut-street, eating my roll all the way, and, coming round, found myself again at Market-street wharf, near the boat I came in, to which I

Philadelphia in 1735 about ten years after Benjamin Franklin's arrival.

went for a draught of the river water; and, being filled with one of my rolls, gave the other two to a woman and her child that came down the river in the boat with us, and were waiting to go farther.

Thus refreshed, I walked again up the street, which by this time had many clean-dressed people in it, who were all walking the same way. I joined them, and thereby was led into the great meeting-house of the Quakers near the market. I sat down among them, and, after looking round awhile and hearing nothing said, being very drowsy thro' labor and want of rest the preceding night, I fell fast asleep, and continu'd so till the meeting broke up, when one was kind enough to rouse me. This was, therefore, the first house I was in, or slept in, in Philadelphia.

Benjamin Franklin

Franklin on Friendship

*Be slow in choosing a friend,
slower in changing.*

*Thou can'st not joke an enemy into a friend,
but thou may'st a friend into an enemy.*

*When befriended, remember it:
When you befriend, forget it.*

*Friendship increases by visiting friends,
but by visiting seldom.*

*A brother may not be a friend,
but a friend will always be a brother.*

*Friendship cannot live with ceremony,
nor without civility.*

Friends are the true scepters of princes.

If you would be loved, love and be lovable.

The Signing of the Declaration

When outraged citizens renounced the hand
Of despot's rule and brutal tyranny
Two hundred years ago in our great land,
Brave energetic men made history...
A Declaration was to set them free.
No longer would Americans delay
Or to a potentate pledge loyalty.
The time had come and they would have their say
For freedom and for independence on that day.
Thus, on a ne'er forgotten afternoon
John Hancock signed the famous document.
The quill was passed in that historic room
And one by one, they signed without dissent...
The deed was done, the hour had been well spent.
They stood prepared for opposition's storm,
Let come what may, they never would relent.
All foreign interference they would scorn,
For now a nation in a new world had been born.

Elsie Natalie Brady

Painting opposite
POSTING THE DECLARATION
by Francis Chase

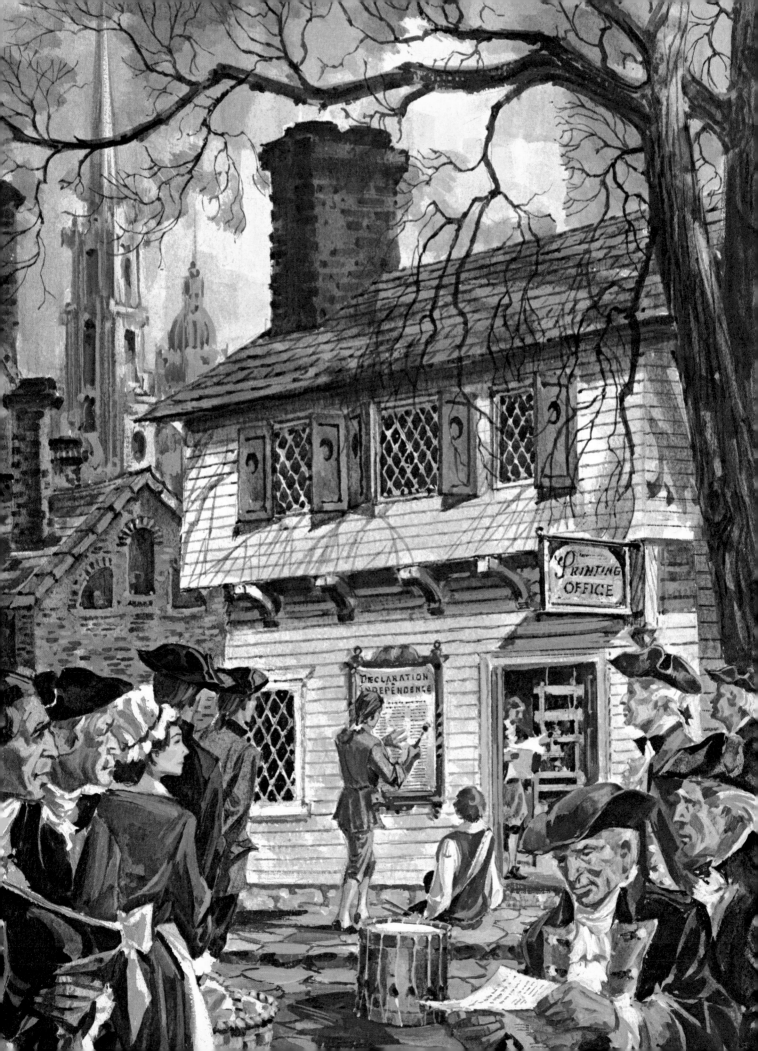

What is an American?

Harold W. Ruopp

An American ... is one who believes in the right of men and women of whatever creed, class, color or ancestry to live as human beings with the dignity becoming the children of God.

An American ... is one who believes in the right to be free; free not only from crushing coercions of dictatorships and regimentation, but free for that way of life where men may think and speak as they choose and worship God as they see fit.

An American ... is one who believes in the right to vote, the right to work, the right to learn, the right to live and, what is equally important, in the right to be different; for he knows that if we ever lose the right to be different we lose the right to be free.

An American ... is one who believes in democracy, not only for himself but for all his fellow-Americans. By democracy he means not simply the rule of

It summoned a meeting of patriots on April 27, 1775, after the Battle of Lexington.

It took its first journey from Philadelphia to Allentown, Pennsylvania, in September, 1775, to escape capture by the British.

It proclaimed the "Birth of a new nation" on July 8, 1776.

It was returned from Allentown on June 27, 1778.

It announced the surrender of Cornwallis at Yorktown on October 24, 1781.

It proclaimed the treaty of peace on April 16, 1783.

It tolled for the death of George Washington on December 20, 1799.

It was rung on the 50th anniversary of the Declaration of Independence on July 4, 1826.

It cracked in the tolling for the death of John Marshall on July eighth, 1835.

the majority but the rights of minorities; and those minorities have rights, not because they are minorities, but because they are human beings.

An American . . . is one who believes in the responsibility of privilege. What he asks for himself, he is willing to grant to others; what he demands from others, he is willing to give himself. His creed is not alone, "Live and let live," but "Live and help live."

An American . . . is one who acts from faith in others, not fear of others; from understanding, not prejudice; from goodwill, not hatred. To bigotry he gives no sanction; to intolerance no support.

The true American never asks, "Are you a Protestant or Catholic, Gentile or Jew, white or colored, but, are you an American? If you are, then give me your hand, for I am an American too."

Reprinted from Baylor Progress,
Baylor University Medical Center.
Used by permission.

The Day Our Nation Came of Age

The heat of the long summer of 1787 lingered over Philadelphia. The big man at the desk in the State House ran a nervous finger under his neckband and picked up the quill. For a moment he stared at the document before him. Then with a trembling hand he scrawled his signature . . . *Go. Washington.*

As thirty-eight men came forward to sign their names, a sense of wonderment grew in his mind. Wonderment at how these men, so varied in their political thinking, had come to agree on something so tangible that it lay there on the desk in black and white—a Constitution, created out of months of bitter controversy behind closed doors.

He remembered that terrible day in June, when the room had been filled with angry voices. The little states were afraid of the big states. Bluntly, Gunning Bedford, Delaware's delegate, had shouted the words. There could be no compromise.

Tempers flared so high that, at the suggestion of wise old Benjamin Franklin, they had adjourned for three days to cool off. And when they came back, the men who had spurned compromise, accepted the Connecticut plan, striking a balance between large and small states. Then they had gone on to forge the other imperishable words in this document of freedom.

"We the People . . ." Washington wondered if *they*, like the men in this room, would realize that the Constitution held America's one bright hope for the future? While the thirty-eight other signers stepped forward to add their names, he watched with absorbed interest.

Here were young men, old men, men of property, men of toil, some born in the British Isles, some in America. And now came the last signer, Abraham Baldwin of Georgia, kindly-faced lawyer. "God has willed that we make this instrument for the people," he had said.

Washington felt a great surge of reassurance. A miracle had occurred here. If these men could agree then, surely, so could the people. One of Washington's rare smiles crossed his face as he put an arm about the stooped shoulders of Franklin. At last he knew, beyond all doubt, that a great nation had come of age.

Madelyn Wood

O beautiful for spacious skies, for amber waves of grain,
For purple mountain majesty above the fruited plain . . .

More Than the Hills

Loving America, what do we love?
For each there is one region where the earth
Seems firmer underfoot, and the sky above
Much larger, and the taste of grief and mirth
More pungent, the ideal more near at hand
Than elsewhere in the broad, beloved land.

But it is all beloved. We who grow
To fit the Smoky Mountains' misty heights
Are larger for the Mississippi's flow,
The prairies' sweep, the star-keen desert nights . . .
For knowing there is one vast dream we share
With folk in all the vastness, everywhere.

America! America! God shed His grace on thee,
And crown thy good with brotherhood from sea to shining sea.

Katherine Lee Bates

Each one of us, in all the diverse space,
Is inwardly at home, because we each
Are native to the dream more than the place,
The mighty dream of goals all men may reach,
The boundless vision of what men may be . . .
The land is where we set the vision free.

We love the land because we love the dream
Of justice and of liberty for all,
Of each heart free to follow its own gleam
To its own victory, erect and tall.
More than the hills, the rivers, or the loam
Of any region, the vision is our home.

Jane Merchant

From HALFWAY UP THE SKY by Jane Merchant.
Poem copyright © 1956 assigned to Abingdon Press.

Earth, thou great footstool of our God, who reigns
on high...thou fruitful source of all our raiment, life,
and food...our house, our parent, and our nurse.

Isaac Watts

New England Village

Little towns, hovering sedately upon a rockbound coast,
Nestled in mountain valleys or upon hills serene,
In your narrow streets, in churches and gabled mansions
A nation began her destiny, found her dream.

Yes, America's dream began along harbor quays,
In stagecoach inns beneath quaint overhanging eaves,
On village greens where the first colonial minutemen
Fought for freedom beneath sun-splashed April trees.

Today, the patina of that past uniquely clings
To gift shop, lighthouse, tearoom, country store,
To gardens where beach plum, shadbush, magnolia, bayberry
Bloom near Atlantic's whisper or titanic roar.

Wineglass elms adorn picturesque winding roads,
Each night, peach-tinted windows beckon with friendly glow
Whether in summer, amid the beauty of leaf and blossom,
Or in winter when the land is caressed by shimmering snow.

From church spires, chimes ring gently over street and lawn,
Over garden and orchard dreaming in golden sunset light,
Over harbors where boats are anchored in shining waters
And gulls on silver wings soar into graceful flight.

Cherry and apple blossoms garland each lane and orchard
Where orioles call and lark or brown thrush sings,
Lilacs diffuse sweet fragrance over gate and picket fence
Where sparrow, wren and robin rest weary wings.

Summer fields are bright with daisies, gentians, goldenrod,
Or redolent with new-mown hay, wild rose and clover,
Katydids and crickets hum among poppies, larkspur, phlox,
And in azure skies are heard wild duck, crow and plover.

Sea captains' homes ornate with cupola and widow's walk,
Ships challenging the ceaseless might of ocean tides,
Shining windows radiating welcome to both friend and stranger
Reflect America's gallantry, hospitality and pride.

From streets that knew the horrendous war cry of the Iroquois
Above brandished tomahawks in glades beyond stockade wall,
Colonists marched to defend a nation's irradiant dream
And, with immortal courage, answer freedom's martial call.

Little villages, you knew the steps of those mighty ones
Who fought for liberty with valorous sword and pen,
The names of Washington, Franklin, Lafayette are enshrined
With those of Emerson, Thoreau, Whittier in the hearts of men.

New England village, whether cosily ensconced in Berkshire vale
Or courageously facing the endless onrush of the sea,
To America, you will ever be a treasured inspiration,
Epitomizing the ageless valor that made her free.

Winifred Marie Burdick

New England Coast

Julia Lott

My heart has need of vast tranquillities
    That quiet meadows keep in constant store:
Pink shells that sing of caves beneath the seas,
    Deep waters murmuring along the shore,
Sweet grass that yields an incense to the air,
    The cleaving prows of ships, the flying spray,
The ebbing tide, these daisies white and fair,
    And gulls that dip above the sheltered bay.

My heart is soothed by these unhurried things;
    I hold them close — I can again go down
Remembering the peaceful lift of wings,
    The silhouette of sails beyond the town,
And how at dusk the lighthouse beacon gleams
    When night is blue upon this shore of dreams.

Sea Call

Ruth Garrison Scurlock

I'm a rover born;
I wake to the horn
That is blown by the young
   sea wind,
And my heart beats in tune,
For I know that I'll soon
Take the path to the
   dawn-trail's end.

Rocking ships that ride
   on the main,
Wind-swept cliffs and
   tropical rain;
Paths to Cathay
Call me today,
I'm off on the long trek again.

The heart of a lass
Holds love that will pass,
But the love of the sea
   holds true.
And the song I sing
Is of the grey gull's wing
And the depths of the
   sea road's blue.

Longwood Mansion

Construction on Longwood, the largest octagonal house in the United States began prior to the Civil War and was halted at the outbreak of the conflict. Dominated by a huge cupola this five-story mansion remains unfinished, with the exception of the nine-room ground floor, furnished in the style of the 1840's. This interesting home has been designated as a National Historic Landmark.

The South

The South was the first America, older than any of the other areas that would make up the United States, predating Puritan New England or Dutch New York or the Pennsylvania of the Quakers. It was the meeting place of three great cultures—Anglo-Saxon, Spanish, and French; and several of their clashes within its borders shaped the course of New World development.

Here was an opulent land, with towering forests and ripe vegetation that approached the tropical. Much of it had a climate of burning sun and violent rain that nurtured a great potential agricultural wealth, with a crop season that lasted through eight or nine months of the year.

The locale fostered a somnolent mood. Under warm skies, across a fragrant humid earth, men moved slowly, riding casually and living most of their days in the open—in the afternoon shadow when possible, on a wide porch by preference. From its beginning to its end, the Old South had largely a rural cast.

Endless green plains, the rolling Bluegrass Country of Kentucky, the clay hills of Georgia and Mississippi, dreaming Louisiana bayous, high river bluffs at Natchez and Vicksburg . . . the Old South encompassed them all.

In Florida and Texas, Spanish elements contributed to the richness of the region, and in the Mississippi Valley the French left tangible evidences of their presence in style and spirit. But in general the South received much the same settlers, in much the same classes, as did other parts of the future United States.

For such plantation people, a bountiful land fostered a bountiful manner of existence: a wide-handed welcome to friend, genial hospitality for strangers, hours of casual enjoyment. Some have argued that this capacity to appreciate leisure might be counted among the Old South's major accomplishments. With it went a related ability, the art of good talk.

Harnett T. Kane

From the book GONE ARE THE DAYS by Harnett T. Kane. Copyright ©1960 by Harnett T. Kane. Published by E. P. Dutton & Co., Inc. and used with their permission

The South in the Springtime

The South in the springtime is a bright carnival
Of flowers on a carpet of green neath a sky of blue;
An apple, plum, and peach blossom festival;
An endless trail of azaleas in every vivid hue.

White dogwood, pink camellias, sweet honeysuckle,
Roses, magnolia, and bridal wreaths abundantly grow
Where the petals of lavender crepe myrtle,
When fallen, weave an intricate blanket of purple snow.

Evelyn Long

*From WORTH REMEMBERING by Evelyn Long.
Copyright 1965 by Evelyn Long. Reprinted
by permission of Exposition Press, Inc.,
Hicksville, N.Y. 11801*

I know of no lovelier place on earth
Than the South when the fragile blossoming
Of peach and pear and plum is brought to birth
Upon greening hills by the warmth of spring.
Nor could there be a fairer sight to see
Than violets trimming her crystal streams
While dogwoods spread their white embroidery
And the redbuds thrill us with cerise gleams.
Silver satin clouds drift in turquoise skies,
Birds become ecstatic with songs of praise;
Up from valleys, amethystine mists rise
And azaleas pink-fringe the woodland ways.
Surely no one could ever ask for more
Than the South with white lilacs at the door

Earle J. Grant

Stanton Hall was the most palatial mansion
built during the great cotton era in Natchez.
The builder of Stanton Hall chartered a ship
to bring materials and furnishings from Europe
for his new home. Further importations from
abroad were made during the five years the
house was under construction. From England
came handsome solid-silver hinges, knobs and
key plates for the doors and from Italy came
lacy iron grillwork by the ton for the porches.
Indoors no expense was spared for the mantels
of white Carrara marble or the bronze French
chandeliers hanging from twenty-two foot high
ceilings.

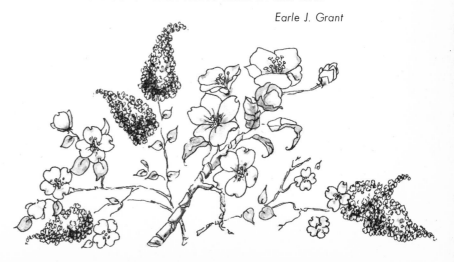

The Wind Across the Prairie

Cassie Eugenia Tartoué

The wind across the prairie
Plays a melancholy air
Through the harp strings of the grass;
It breathes a soulful prayer
Against vermilion boulders,
It ripples fields of grain
Into shimmering lakes of green and gold,
And bears the scent of rain.

The wind across the prairie
With organ-voicéd sigh
Sings a hymn to all the rangeland
In the haze of earth and sky.
The lonely horseman ponders
As he feels the wind's soft breath,
The grandeur of the prairie
And its song of life and death.

The wind across the prairie,
Like a sculptor's careful hand
Carves upon the earth and stone
The splendor of the land.
With a voice both cruel and tender,
It sings its song of time,
And bends aside the mundane things
To show us the sublime.

©

FADING MEMORIES OF THE FAMILY FARM

Jay Scriba

Someday soon the old family farm will be nothing but a dark stain in the leached clay of somebody's cornfield. There will be nothing for the archeologist but the caved in brick wells, with the rusty Galena pumps fallen in time's burial. For the moment, though, the locust grove still rises like a green island, with the weather-beaten clapboard house sagging in a thicket of ragweed and tansy...

On our last visit, the only sign of recent human habitation was in the smokehouse, where Aunt Grace's patched chore sweater still hung on a nail, just where she left it when the weariness of eighty-five years forced her to "rent a little place in town."

She was the last of the old folks, still living on a little eighty acre farm which, even in the 1940s, was run with kerosene lamps, a horse-drawn corn plow and cobs burned in the kitchen stove. When we visited during summer vacations, there were still

trunks in the attic, left from the family's immigrant trip from Sweden in the 1880s.

For a restless town boy, nothing could match the thrill of a couple of July weeks on the old farm. You awoke to crowing roosters, opening an eye to sun streaming through the cracks in the green shades. Even the bedding was different... a patchwork quilt over a rustling corn shuck mattress and embroidery on the feather pillows (smelling richly of the hen house).

The aunts and uncles, of course, had been up since dawn, milking cows, watering chickens, digging into the lard crock for pre-fried pork sausage patties, pungent with pepper and sage. There was a smell of Swedish pot coffee, a sound of soft farm talk from the kitchen. Sometimes the milk on our oatmeal was still warm and foaming from the cow.

What to do first? Uncle Charley was hoeing among the sweet corn and cucumbers, stopping now and then to file a bright edge. Later he would be puttering in the garage, where a Kentucky rifle still hung on the wall, over a collection of license plates dating back to 1914.

Aunt Grace was pumping one of the old Galenas, filling the smokehouse trough with cold water to cool the milk, butter and cottage cheese, fresh from the back of the kitchen stove.

Aunt Mary had put on a sunbonnet and stretched silk stockings over her arms to protect them from brambles on a blackberrying expedition to Burton's woods. (One of several dark, grape tangled, oak and hickory groves left from the great clearing after the Civil War. "Indian groves," Uncle Charley called them.)

For a start, we generally went off on our own, out to the barnyard to pump the pig and horse troughs full, eager to pat a snuffling mare on her velvet nose. The little pigs were warier, standing stiff legged and alert, set for playful, squealing flight at the wave of a new straw hat.

We might go into the corncrib in the new red barn to shell a few ears in the racketing hand sheller. Or we might climb into the heaped wheat in the grain bin... the most comfortable lounging cushion in the world... and chew a handful of kernels until they became a chaffy gum.

Continued

For heart-pounding excitement, we visited the hog house, where a surly five-hundred pound brood sow in the shadows made the place seem as menacing as a lion pit. ("Hey, you, get in there and she'll eat you to the bone!") There was also an ornery cow that Uncle Charley had named W.F.M.S. . . . for Women's Foreign Missionary Society . . . who would charge you like a ring bull. One Leghorn rooster was mean, too, an immensely haughty creature, the epitome of that description of a young sport heading for a dance as "steppin' out like a rooster in high oats."

Through the rest of the morning we might ride on one of the big horses while Uncle Charley plowed corn, clinging desperately to the fly netting as Big Jack shook his hide to dislodge a horsefly. The thing to do was grip hard on brass collar balls and never look down.

Then it would be noon, with Aunt Grace ringing a cowbell. Time to go to the rain barrel, swat the wash pan hard to drive down the swarming mosquito wigglers and wash up, maybe sticking your cowlick under the icy pump water. (The wooden pump deck stood among moss, wild mint and the purple flowers of gill on the ground.)

Dinner was substantial, with dark slices of smoked ham down from the attic, bowls of mashed potatoes with cream gravy, watermelon pickles, spiced peaches, iced tea, a firm flaky slice of cherry or apple pie. (Always by 11 a.m. a pie cooling in the kitchen window.)

After the pie there was time for a nap on the creaking porch swing, next to the sweet honeysuckle, or in the hammock, next to the truck patch (gooseberries, currants, chives, asparagus, a gourmet's dream of fresh vegetables).

The ninety-degree afternoon heat might find us with an oil can, filling the cups on a dilapidated corn planter, mower and other machinery in the implement shed. We would hunt eggs by the hour in the tangled goldenrod and jimsonweed, sometimes returning in triumph with whole clutches.

By four o'clock it was time for coffee and a slice of pink iced angel cake. Aunt Mary would be back with a milk pail full of glistening blackberries. Uncle Charley would tell Aunt Grace that the wind had shifted west and that it was "darkening up" . . . a signal for everybody to get out and shoo the half-

wild Plymouth Rock hens into a dozen weathered lean-tos.

As farmer readers have already surmised, the old folks seldom saw anything larger than a five dollar bill. But what is poverty when there are bushels of potatoes in the root cellar and flitches of bacon hanging in the smokehouse? The milk and eggs always provided enough for a new pair of "gum boots," a pledge to the church, a quart of vanilla ice cream from the supply store. (Mixed, on Sunday afternoon after the croquet game, with homemade root beer to make "black cow" sodas.)

Evening came with a flight of hundreds of crows, beating for a roosting woods beyond the sleepy river. You began to hear farmers calling their hogs, Ben Osborn's "Whoooeeeee!," burly Levi Holst's bawling "Wheeeeaaaaww!" There was a great

squealing rush of pigs as Uncle Charley banged corn ears into a metal bushel, poured slop into the wooden hog trough. Then it was time for milking, with the white streams ringing in the pails, the one-eyed farm cats creeping in for their enameled pan of frothy largesse.

We would hang on the Dutch barn door, watching the shadows slant over the miles of cornfields, listening to the slow creak of the vine-covered windmill. Sometimes we turned the crank on the milk separator, winding it to a high whine.

Supper was in the soft dark, under a fake Tiffany kerosene lamp with an irresistible glass bead fringe. For a while we would sit on the lawn with Uncle Charley, smelling the hot hay wind while he picked fat ticks off his tail-thumping "shepherd" dog. Aunt Grace had already begun to yawn before she put on her reading spectacles and sat down with the crossword puzzle or her worn Bible. Half an hour and she began to snore, not a nerve twitching in the peace of her tired soul. By now Uncle Charley, who lived in town, had bumped his Model A down the grassy lane, leaving the locust grove steeped in quiet and the beep of katydids.

Nobody would set an alarm clock in a countryside full of boastful roosters. By nine o'clock a strange, delicious weariness made it easy for even a fidgeting boy to unlace his tennis shoes, put aside his copy of *Black Beauty* or the *The Bobbsey Twins at the Farm*.

It wasn't until years later that we realized how lucky we were to have savored the good, simple people, the last years of a pioneer pocket in the American Middle West.

Out Where the West Begins

Out where the handclasp's a little stronger,
Out where the smile dwells a little longer,
That's where the West begins;
Out where the sun is a little brighter,
Where the snows that fall are a trifle whiter,
Where the bonds of home are a wee bit tighter...
That's where the West begins.

Out where the skies are a trifle bluer,
Out where friendship's a little truer,
That's where the West begins;
Out where a fresher breeze is blowing,
Where there's laughter in every streamlet flowing,
Where there's more of reaping and less of sowing...
That's where the West begins.

Out where the world is in the making,
Where fewer hearts in despair are aching,
That's where the West begins;
Where there's more of singing and less of sighing,
Where there's more of giving and less of buying,
And a man makes friends without half trying...
That's where the West begins.

Arthur Chapman

PORTRAITS OF THE OLD WEST

Three great Americans write about a part of vanished America— the Old West. The first, Mark Twain, describes the beginning of a stagecoach journey from St. Joseph, Missouri to Nevada in July, 1861.

Another way to the West

OVERLAND BY STAGE

The first thing we did on that glad evening that landed us at St. Joseph was to hunt up the stage-office, and pay a hundred and fifty dollars apiece for tickets per overland coach to Carson City, Nevada.

The next morning, bright and early, we took a hasty breakfast, and hurried to the starting-place . . . By eight o'clock everything was ready, and we were on the other side of the river. We jumped into the stage, the driver cracked his whip, and we bowled away and left "the States" behind us. It was a superb summer morning, and all the landscape was brilliant with sunshine. There was a freshness and breeziness, too, and an exhilarating sense of emancipation from all sorts of cares and responsibilities, that almost made us feel that the years we had spent in the close, hot city, toiling and slaving, had been wasted and thrown away. We were spinning along through Kansas, and in the course of an hour and a half we were fairly abroad on the great Plains. Just here the land was rolling—a grand sweep of regular elevations and depressions as far as the eye could reach—like the stately heave and swell of the ocean's bosom after a storm. And everywhere were cornfields, accenting with squares of deeper green, this limitless expanse of grassy land. But presently this sea upon dry ground was to lose its "rolling" character and stretch away for seven hundred miles as level as a floor!

Our coach was a great swinging and swaying stage, of the most sumptuous description—an imposing cradle on wheels. It was drawn by six handsome horses, and by the side of the driver sat the "conductor," the legitimate captain of the craft; for it was his business to take charge and care of the mails, baggage, express matter, and passengers. We three were the only passengers, this trip. We sat on the back seat, inside. About all the rest of the coach was full of mail bags—for we had three days' delayed mails with us. Almost touching our knees, a perpendicular wall of mail matter rose up to the roof. There was a great pile of it strapped on top of the stage, and both the fore and hind boots were full.

We changed horses every ten miles, all day long, and fairly flew over the hard, level road. We jumped out and stretched our legs every time the coach stopped, and so the night found us still vivacious and unfatigued.

Excerpts abridged from pp. 4, 6, 7 and 9 ROUGHING IT by Mark Twain (Harper & Row)

An advocate of western expansion and a champion of a transcontinental railroad, Horace Greeley journeyed across America in 1859 from New York to San Francisco to see firsthand the fabled and largely unexplored territory of the West. This famous editor of the New York Tribune recorded impressions of his travels in a series of articles for the newspaper. Below are the observations of Greeley who advised: "Go West, young man, and grow up with the country."

LAST OF THE BUFFALO

I would rather not bore the public with buffalo. I fully realize that the subject is not novel—that Irving, and Cooper, and many others, have written fully and admirably upon it; and that the traveler's enthusiastic recital falls coldly on the ear of the distant, critical, unsympathizing reader. Yet I insist on writing this once more on buffalo, promising then to drop the subject, as we pass out of the range of the buffalo before night. All day yesterday, they darkened the earth around us, often seeming to be drawn up like an army in battle array on the ridges and adown their slopes a mile or so south of us—often on the north as well. They are rather shy of the little screens of straggling timber on the creek bottoms—doubtless from their sore experience of Indians lurking therein to discharge arrows at them as they went down to drink. If they feed in the grass of the narrow valleys and ravines, they are careful to have a part of the herd on the ridges which overlook them, and with them the surrounding country for miles. And, when an alarm is given, they all rush furiously off in the direction which the leaders presume that of safety.

What strikes the stranger with most amazement is their immense numbers. I know a million is a great many, but I am confident we saw that number yesterday. Certainly, all we saw could not have stood on ten square miles of ground. Often, the country for miles on either hand seemed quite black with them. The soil is rich, and well matted with their favorite grass. Yet it is all (except a very little on the creek bottoms, near to timber) eaten down like an overtaxed sheep pasture in a dry August. Consider that we have traversed more than one hundred miles in width since we first struck them, and that for most of this distance the buffalo have been constantly in sight, and that they continue for some twenty-five miles further on—this being the breadth of their present range, which has a length of perhaps a thousand miles—and you have some approach to an idea of their countless myriads.

Horace Greeley

The Oregon Trail

Two hundred wagons, rolling out to Oregon
  Breaking through the gopher holes, lurching wide and free,
Crawling up the mountain pass, jolting, grumbling, rumbling on,
  Two hundred wagons, rolling to the sea.

From east and south and north they flock, to muster, row on row,
A fleet of ten-score prairie ships beside Missouri's flow.
The bullwhips crack, the oxen strain, the canvas-hooded files
Are off upon the long, long trail of sixteen hundred miles.
The women hold the guiding lines; beside the rocking steers
With goad and ready rifle walk the bearded pioneers
Through clouds of dust beneath the sun, through floods of sweeping rain
Across the Kansas prairie land, across Nebraska's plain.

Two hundred wagons, rolling out to Oregon,
  Curved around the campfire flame at halt when day is done,
Rest a while beneath the stars, yoke again and lumber on,
  Two hundred wagons, rolling with the sun.

Among the barren buttes they wind beneath the jealous view
Of Blackfoot, Pawnee, Omaha, Arapahoe, and Sioux.
No savage threat may check their course, no river deep and wide;
They swim the Platte, they ford the Snake, they cross the Great Divide.
They march as once from India's vales through Asia's mountain door
With shield and spear on Europe's plain their fathers marched before.
They march where leap the antelope and storm the buffalo,
Still westward as their fathers marched ten thousand years ago.

Two hundred wagons, rolling out to Oregon
  Creeping down the dark defile below the mountain crest,
Surging through the brawling stream, lunging, plunging, forging on,
  Two hundred wagons, rolling toward the West.

Now toils the dusty caravan with swinging wagon poles
Where Walla Walla pours along, where broad Columbia rolls.
The long-haired trapper's face grows dark and scowls the painted brave;
Where now the beaver builds his dam the wheat and rye shall wave.
The British trader shakes his head and weighs his nation's loss,
For where those hardy settlers come the Stars and Stripes will toss.
Then block the wheels, unyoke the steers; the prize is his who dares;
The cabins rise, the fields are sown, and Oregon is theirs!

          They will take, they will hold,
          By the spade in the mold,
          By the seed in the soil,
          By the sweat and the toil,
          By the plow in the loam,
          By the school and the home!

Two hundred wagons, rolling out to Oregon,
  Two hundred wagons, ranging free and far,
Two hundred wagons, rumbling, grumbling, rolling on,
  Two hundred wagons, following a star!

Arthur Guiterman

Our Country

This great broad land of ours: its sweeping plains,
Its rivers deep and long, its mountain chains,
Enchant my enraptured heart with joy and pride
And set me roving free from tide to tide.

I love its snow-clad peaks, its lakes of blue,
Its golden dawnings and its morning dew;
I cherish every road that leads me far
Toward crimson sunset and bright evening star.

I've known its summer heat, its winter cold,
As through its length and breadth I've gaily strolled.
I've seen it stretched below as from the air
I've watched it, like a man, unroll down there.

Its flowering desert sands, its mighty trees,
I've taken to my heart as one who sees
Them as his gifts from God whose lavish hand
Has decked with living gems this lovely land.

Oh, would that all who live within its bound
Could realize that they're on holy ground,
And that our lives would then as comely be
As is America . . . land of the free.

Lewis Parker Miller

Mount Rushmore

The President placed a drill in the hands of a stocky, energetic man. The tool bit deep into granite. Thus in 1927 did Calvin Coolidge, self-conscious in a ten-gallon hat, launch the work of sculptor Gutzon Borglum upon the face of Mount Rushmore in South Dakota.

For 14 summers mountain foliage—pine, spruce, silver birch, aspen—shuddered to the blast of dynamite, the chatter of jackhammer. When the last stone fragment tumbled from the mountain, stillness settled over the valley. Carved from this Western Gibraltar stood the world's most heroic sculpture.

"Trained but not tamed," men said of Idaho-born Borglum. A famed disciple of Rodin in Paris, he was a man of many enthusiasms—writer, engineer, an impatient patriot. "There is not a monument in the country as big as a snuff box," he said in 1916. America demanded "an enlarged dimension—a new scale."

Borglum found that scale, and a challenge for all his talents, when historian Doane Robinson suggested a monumental sculpture in the Black Hills. Near the town of Keystone the sculptor examined an exposed granite core. The southeastern face of 5,725-foot Mount Rushmore offered greatest promise. Private funds, then Federal appropriations got the job underway.

Borglum fashioned plaster models, measured them, then dropped proportionate plumb lines from the mountain-top. Faces would be sixty feet tall—as high as a five-story building. Dynamite shots probed reliable rock beneath the deeply fissured surface. Nine times Borglum remade his models to conform to solid stone. He climbed scaffolds training miners to help him; he darted about the canyon to test the effect of shadow upon a cheek or chin.

First face to be completed was, appropriately, George Washington's. Next emerged Thomas Jefferson, eyes fixed on the horizon his Louisiana Purchase had assured. Brow-first, Abraham Lincoln took shape, melancholy in his mission to keep America intact. Last, with a square jaw apt in granite, Theodore Roosevelt's image evoked the vigor of twentieth-century America. But Gutzon Borglum did not live to see his masterpiece complete; he died at seventy-four, leaving seven month's work to the son he had named for Lincoln.

"I don't intent that it shall be just a three-day tourist wonder," Borglum once said. Tourists themselves, a million a year, testify to his success. They stop in hotels and motor courts in Rapid City and Keystone, South Dakota. In holiday mood they picnic in nearby Black Hills National Forest or feast in the attractive restaurant at the Rushmore site itself.

They come not to gaze at a giant curiosity, but to observe a monument as large and permanent as the dream these four men made real. Some return time and again to watch morning sunlight move across the faces, to see the figures backed by a Western sunset, to attend the nightly summer ceremony in the amphitheater as floodlights whiten the granite against a black sky.

At whatever time of day, the setting inspires an inward awe. Frank Lloyd Wright left aside all his brilliant barbs when he saw Rushmore: "The noble countenances emerge as though the spirit of the mountain heard a human plan and itself became a human countenance." Vacationers, freshly conscious of the meaning of citizenship, say even more by their reflective silence.

Bart McDowell

Heritage

No gold or jewels have I to give you,
But I give you the joy of sunshine,
The indescribable beauty of a sunset,
Nodding daffodils,
Birdsongs to cheer a weary heart,
Quiet brooks that mirror the reflection of the forest trees,
The night sky candles that twinkle . . .
The hearty laugh of a little child,
Stalwart pines, snow-covered,
The watchful moon,
The humble violet,
The diligent squirrel . . .
Spring rains, warm and dripping,
Alluring cherry blossoms,
The look of confidence in a dog's eyes,
A soothing, singing breeze . . . the brilliant rainbow,
A task to perform,
Sadness and tears, too, that teach us to keep the faith.
These things I give to you . . .
A heritage far dearer than gold or jewels.

LaVetta L. Hummel

There Is This Land

Ruby Lee Mitchell

There is this land, this great wonderful land
Where beauty lies on almost every hand,
And rich grains grow in countless spreading fields
And spill their bounty in redundant yields
　of plenty for its people.

There is this land of mountains, rivers, plains,
Whose cities, suburbs, have growing pains.
And there is wide deep country, quiet, still,
And peace to be found by a singing rill . . .
This land has everything and it is mine!

Here deep in my heart I feel its design,
Its deep-rooted desire to keep us free,
This shining land reaching from sea to sea.
There is this land of forests, boundless, tall,
And snows and burning sun and rich rainfall;
Land of mansions, huts and churches with spires
Pointing skyward, tempering man's desires . . .

A kaleidoscope of races and creeds,
A magnitude of magnificent deeds.
This is our land and all of us born free . . .
Freedom burns now and will forever be,
Its candle-flame by patriotism fanned . . .
Oh, God, our God, we thank Thee for this land!

Prayer for the United States of America

George Washington

Almighty God, we make our earnest prayer that Thou wilt keep the United States in Thy holy protection; that Thou wilt incline the hearts of the citizens to cultivate a spirit of subordination and obedience to government . . . And finally that Thou wilt most graciously be pleased to dispose us all to do justice, to love mercy and to demean ourselves with that charity, humility and pacific temper of mind which were the characteristics of the Divine Author of our blessed religion, and without a humble imitation of whose example in these things we can never hope to be a happy nation. Grant our supplication, we beseech Thee, through Jesus Christ our Lord. Amen.

In God We Trust

Author Unknown

The path we travel is narrow and long, beset with many dangers. Each day we must ask that Almighty God will set and keep His protecting hand over us so that we may pass on to those who come after us the heritage of a free people, secure in their God-given rights and in full control of a government dedicated to the preservation of those rights. Without God, there could be no American form of government, nor an American way of life . . . thus the Founding Fathers saw it; and thus, with God's help, it will continue to be.

Give me your tired, your poor, your huddled masses yearning to breathe free. The wretched refuse of your teeming shore, send these; the homeless, tempest-tossed to me. I lift the lamp beside the golden door.

Emma Lazarus
Inscription on the Statue of Liberty

Our Flag

A. P. Putnam

What precious associations cluster around our flag! Not alone have our fathers set up this banner in the name of God over the well-won battlefields of the Revolution, and over the cities and towns which they rescued from despotic rule, but think where also their descendants have carried it and raised it in conquest or protection. Through what clouds of dust and smoke has it passed! What storms of shot and shell! What scenes of fire and blood! Not only at Saratoga, at Monmouth and at York-town, but at Lundy's Lane and New Orleans, at Buena Vista and Chapultepec.

It is the same glorious old flag which, inscribed with the dying words of Lawrence, "Don't give up the ship!" was hoisted on Lake Erie by Commodore Perry just on the eve of his great national victory; the same old flag which our great chieftain bore in triumph to the proud city of the Aztecs and planted upon the heights of her national palace.

Brave hands raised it above the eternal regions of ice in the Arctic seas, and have set it up on the lofty mountains of the West. Where has it not gone? The pride of its friends and the terror of its foes. What countries and what seas has it not visited? Where has not the American citizen been able to stand beneath its folds and defy the world?

With what joy and exultation seamen and tourists have gazed upon its Stars and Stripes, read in it the history of their nation's glory, received from it the full sense of security, and drawn from it the inspiration of patriotism! By it how many have sworn fealty to their country! What bursts of magnificent eloquence it has called forth from Webster and from Everett! What lyric strains of poetry from Drake and Holmes!

How many heroes its folds have covered in death! How many have lived for it! How many have died for it! How many living and dying have said in their en-thusiastic devotion to its honor, like that young wounded sufferer in the streets of Baltimore, "Oh, the flag! the Stars and Stripes!" And wherever that flag has gone, it has been the herald of a better day, it has been the pledge of freedom, of jus-tice, of order, of civilization, and of Christianity. Tyrants only have hated it, and the enemies of mankind alone have trampled it to the earth. All who sigh for the triumph of truth and righteousness love and salute it.

*Our sincere thanks to the author
whose address we were unable to locate*

America for Me
Henry van Dyke

'Tis fine to see the Old World,
   and travel up and down
Among the famous palaces and cities
   of renown,
To admire the crumbly castles
   and the statues of the kings,
But now I think I've had enough
   of antiquated things,

So it's home again, and home again,
   America for me!
My heart is turning home again, and there
   I long to be
In the land of youth and freedom
   beyond the ocean bars,
Where the air is full of sunlight and
   the flag is full of stars.

Oh, London is a man's town, there's power
   in the air;
And Paris is a woman's town, with flowers
   in her hair;
And it's sweet to dream in Venice, and
   it's great to study Rome,
But when it comes to living, there is
   no place like home.

I like the German fir-woods, in green
    battalions drilled;
I like the gardens of Versailles with flashing
    fountains filled;
But, oh, to take your hand, my dear,
    and ramble for a day
In the friendly western woodland
    where Nature has her way!

I know that Europe's wonderful, yet
    something seems to lack!
The past is too much with her, and
    the people looking back.
But the glory of the present is to make
    the future free,
We love our land for what she is and what
    she is to be.

Oh, it's home again, and home again,
    America for me!
I want a ship that's westward bound
    to plough the rolling sea,
To the blessed Land of Room Enough
    beyond the ocean bars,
Where the air is full of sunlight and the flag
    is full of stars.

Listen...

Listen to the bells today
Talk of liberty,
Telling us we are great,
And we believe them.
They speak of patriotism
Valley-deep and Mississippi River long.

They shout our courage,
The daily brand
That does not know
The name or color of defeat,
Farmers plowing age-old fields,
Masons laying brick on brick . . .
Everyday stuff that made us what we are.

to the Bells Today

Helen M. Virden

Hear them applaud the schooners going west,
The thud of axes in a virgin wood,
The throb of engines plowing
Unknown seas,
A nation hammered out of grit and steel.

They trumpet stubbornness
As hard as nails,
Determination, oxen-strong
And hickory-tough;
Pour out our pride for Pilgrims
True to creeds;
Chant and cheer for ones
Who newly came
To share this freedom
That men die for . . .

Ring the cadence of our dreams . . .
Our people dream;
Dreams that have bridged mountains,
Hollowed oceans out;
Clang for the bone and sinew
That made them come true
In two short centuries . . .

Fill free air with that brave spirit
Of men who dumped the tyrant's tea,

Who staked their lives and sacred honor
So we might strut this land like kings,
Roam its miles as if they were our
Own backyard
With wheat a golden sea,
Corn, more than the Fourth's knee-high,
Pause to hear their praise
For life and the right to live it . . .

Prove independence here is more
Than just a word,
Make it the bread and meat of our existence,
The one fixed point in this contrary century.

Hear bells ring the clarion call of hope for
What men can aspire to become
When wars are over, prejudice forsaken.

Ring them for yesterday
For all that was brave in it . . .
Ring them for today,
Swirl high this mite of time;
Then let them rock the rafters,
Split the heavens
With the promise of tomorrow
And its hope.

Wear Fifty Stars on the Fourth of July

Mary Lou Kieswetter

The hard-boiled eggs have been deviled, the chicken fried to a golden brown, the potato salad has been seasoned to a gourmet's delight, and Dad's favorite chocolate cake has been frosted an inch deep. The basket bulges as it rides along with an array of lemonade jugs, cameras, and beach balls.

Mom looks ten years younger, with her hair caught back with a gay hair band, and Dad's eyes seem to be more relaxed than I have seen them in months, as he unloads the horseshoes and old catcher's mitt from the station wagon. Yes, according to the number of cars in the parking lot, all America is preparing for play.

You may ask, "What does all of this have to do with our paying tribute to our flag on Independence Day?"

A picnic on Independence Day is America at play. It is Americans celebrating our independence in a great old-fashioned way—a way of casualness that is so true of Americans. It is a way of putting aside our problems, for at least a part of a day.

Perhaps some may say we Americans are too informal in our behavior on this day of our independence—not solemn enough with our tribute to our flag. But I believe patriotism, like religion, need not be formal.

All of us, I am sure, have a special time of day during this celebration when we give our own moment of honor to Old Glory. Perhaps your moment comes at sundown, as mine does, when there is that feeling in the air that seems to be contagious and we all know the big event of the day is still to come. As twilight approaches we find most of America searching the darkened sky for a splash of bright color.

The grandstands and lawns in our parks are filled to capacity with America waiting together to see the final display of the day which signifies the conclusion of another Fourth of July. As the torch is set to the giant framework that supports the American flag display, there is a burst of flaming colors, and a hush of silence gives way to a deafening applause for Old Glory.

Yes, this is what the picnic was all about. It was America at play joined together in one united cause—the cause of honoring our freedom and independence!

Before I leave my home for the day's activities this Fourth of July, I intend to place my flag in its position of honor, at my doorway. As you place your flag on display, step back and take a good look at it. Could you ever put another in its place, or even visualize another color arrangement than the Stars and Stripes? Of course not, but as Americans who have always lived in freedom, we are apt to take this privilege too much for granted. Stop and remember there are thousands of people who desire to take our precious freedom away.

Speak up for our flag, honor it proudly, and you'll be wearing fifty stars in your eyes on the Fourth of July!

The greatest glory of a freeborn people

is to transmit that freedom to their children.

Harvard

Political Religion of America

Abraham Lincoln

Let every American, every lover of liberty, every well-wisher to his posterity, swear by the blood of the Revolution, never to violate in the least particular, the laws of the country, and never tolerate their violation by others. As the patriots of '76 did to the support of the Declaration of Independence, so to the support of the Constitution and laws let every American pledge his life, his property and his sacred honor. Let every man remember that to violate the law is to trample on the blood of his father, and to tear the charter of his own and his children's liberty.

Let reverence for the laws be breathed by every American mother to the lisping babe that prattles on her lap. Let it be taught in the schools, in seminaries and in colleges. Let it be written in primers, spelling-books and in almanacs. Let it be preached from the pulpit, proclaimed in legislative halls, and enforced in courts of justice; and in short, let it become the political religion of the nation. And let the old and the young, the rich and the poor, the grave and the gay of all sexes and tongues and colors and conditions, sacrifice unceasingly upon its altars.

the promise of america

Thomas Wolfe

Go, seeker, if you will, throughout the land and you will find us burning in the night.

There where the hackles of the Rocky Mountains blaze in the blank and naked radiance of the moon, go make your resting stool upon the highest peak. Can you not see us now? The continental wall juts sheer and flat, its huge black shadow on the plain, and the plain sweeps out against the East, two thousand miles away. The great snake that you see there is the Mississippi River.

Behold the gem-strung towns and cities of the good, green East, flung like stardust through the field of night. That spreading constellation to the north is called Chicago, and that giant wink that blazes in the moon is the pendant lake that it is built upon. Beyond, close-set and dense as a clenched fist, are all the jeweled cities of the eastern seaboard. There's Boston, ringed with the bracelet of its shining little towns, and all the lights that sparkle on the rocky indentations of New England. Here, southward and a little to the west, and yet still coasted to the sea, is our intensest ray, the splintered firmament of the towered island of Manhattan. Round about her, sown thick as grain, is the glitter of a hundred towns and cities. The long chain of lights there is the necklace of Long Island and the Jersey shore. Southward and inland, by a foot or two, behold the duller glare of Philadelphia. Southward further still, the twin constellations—Baltimore and Washington. Westward, but still within the borders of the good, green East, that nighttime glow and smolder of hellfire is Pittsburgh. Here, St. Louis, hot and humid in cornfield belly of the land, and bedded on the mid-length coil and fringes of the snake. There at the snake's mouth, southward six hundred miles or so, you see the jeweled crescent of old New Orleans. Here, west and south again, you see the gemmy glitter of the cities on the Texas border.

Turn now, seeker, on your resting stool atop the Rocky Mountains, and look

another thousand miles or so across moon-blazing fiend-worlds of the Painted Desert and beyond Sierras' ridge. That magic congeries of lights there to the west, ringed like a studded belt around the magic setting of its lovely harbor, is the fabled town of San Francisco. Below it, Los Angeles and all the cities of the California shore. A thousand miles to north and west, the sparkling towns of Oregon and Washington.

Observe the whole of it, survey it as you might survey a field. Make it your garden, seeker, or your backyard patch. Be at ease in it. It's your oyster—yours to open if you will. Don't be frightened, it's not so big now, when your footstool is the Rocky Mountains. Reach out and dip a hatful of cold water from Lake Michigan. Drink it—we've tried it—you'll not find it bad. Take your shoes off and work your toes down in the river oozes of the Mississippi bottom—it's very refreshing on a hot night in the summertime. Help yourself to a bunch of Concord grapes up there in northern New York state—they're getting good now. Or raid that watermelon patch down there in Georgia. Or, if you like, you can try the Rocky Fords here at your elbow, in Colorado. Just make yourself at home, refresh yourself, get the feel of things, adjust your sights, and get the scale. It's your pasture now, and it's not so big—only three thousand miles from east to west, only two thousand miles from north to south—but all between, where ten thousand points of light prick out the cities, towns, and villages, there, seeker, you will find us burning in the night.

So, then, to every man his chance—to every man, regardless of his birth, his shining, golden opportunity—to every man the right to live, to work, to be himself, and to become whatever thing his manhood and his vision can combine to make him—this, seeker, is the promise of America.

Breathes there the man with soul so dead
Who never to himself hath said,
　　This is my own, my native land!
Whose heart hath ne'er within him burned,
As home his footsteps he hath turned
　　From wandering on a foreign strand?
If such there breathe, go, mark him well;
For him no minstrel raptures swell;
High though his titles, proud his name,
Boundless his wealth as wish can claim,
Despite those titles, power, and pelf,
The wretch, concentred all in self,
Living, shall forfeit fair renown,
And, doubly dying, shall go down
To the vile dust from whence he sprung,
Unwept, unhonored, and unsung.

Sir Walter Scott

ACKNOWLEDGMENTS

OUT WHERE THE WEST BEGINS by Arthur Chapman. Used through courtesy of the publisher, Houghton Mifflin Company. LAST OF THE BUFFALO by Horace Greeley. This selection was taken from: AN OVERLAND JOURNEY by Horace Greeley, edited and with notes and an introduction by Charles T. Duncan, © 1963 by Alfred A. Knopf, Inc., New York. THE OREGON TRAIL by Arthur Guiterman. From I SING THE PIONEER, published by E. P. Dutton © 1926, © renewed by Vida Lindo Guiterman 1954. FADING MEMORIES OF THE FAMILY FARM by Jay Scriba. Reprinted from THE MILWAUKEE JOURNAL, June 6, 1971. AMERICA by Abba Hillel Silver. Copyrighted. From A TREASURY OF SERMON ILLUSTRATIONS by Abba Hillel Silver. Used by permission of Daniel Jeremy Silver. Our sincere thanks to the following author whose address we were unable to locate for material in this book: LaVetta L. Hummel for HERITAGE.

The Joy of Family

The Joy of Family

A Rutledge Book
The C. R. Gibson Company
Norwalk, Connecticut
U.S.A.

Library of Congress Catalog Card Number 69-17718
SBN 8378-1856-7
Prepared and Produced by Rutledge Books, Inc.
Copyright © MCMLXIX by The C. R. Gibson Company
Norwalk, Connecticut, U.S.A.

We are not born as the partridge in the wood,
or the ostrich of the desert, to be scattered everywhere;
but we are to be grouped together, and brooded
by love, and reared day by day in that first of
churches, the family.

Henry Ward Beecher

Perhaps the greatest blessing in marriage is
that it lasts so long. The years, like the varying
interests of each year, combine to
buttress and enrich each other.

Richard C. Cabot

Marriage resembles a pair of shears, so joined that they cannot be separated: often moving in opposite directions, yet always punishing any one who comes between them.

Sydney Smith

... not a union merely between two creatures ... the
intention of that bond is to perfect the nature of
both, by supplementing their deficiencies with the force
of contrast, giving to each sex those excellences in
which it is naturally deficient ...

Frederick William Robertson

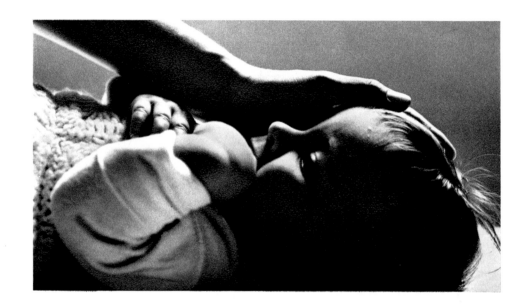

Dependence is a perpetual call upon humanity, and a greater incitement to tenderness and pity than any other motive whatever.

William Makepeace Thackeray

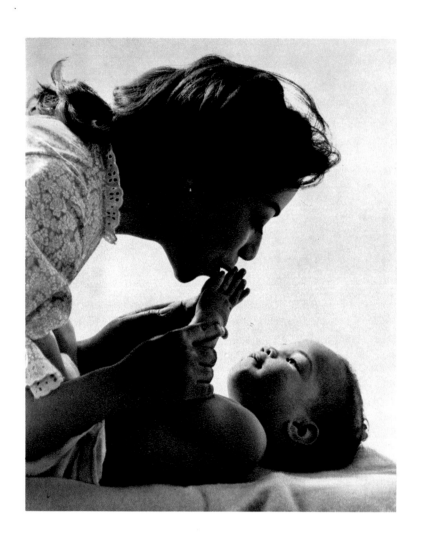

Better to be driven out from among men than to be disliked of children.

Richard Henry Dana

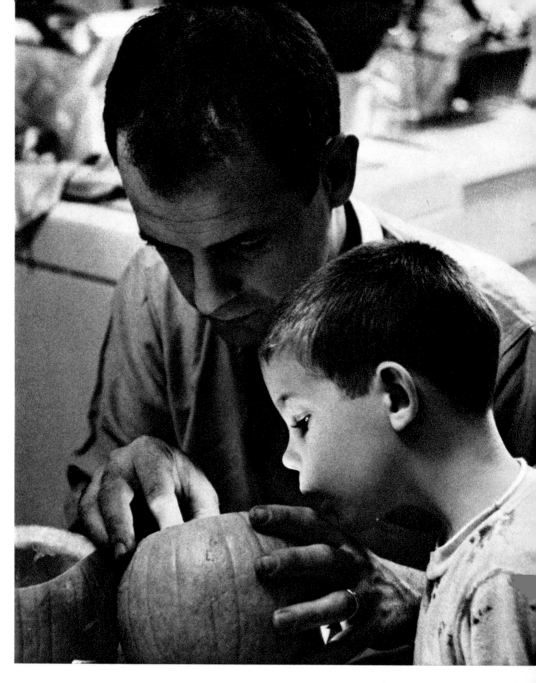

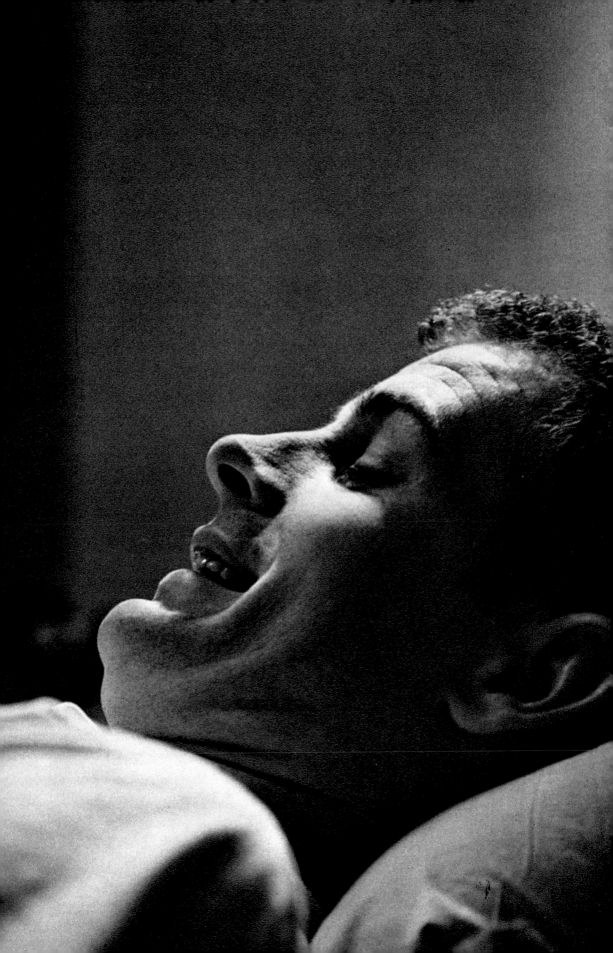

Ye are better than all the ballads
    That ever were sung or said;
For ye are the living poems
    And all the rest are dead.

Henry Wadsworth Longfellow

I have often thought what a melancholy
world this would be without children; and
what an inhuman world, without the aged.

Samuel Taylor Coleridge

So nigh is grandeur to our dust,
   So near is God to man,
When Duty whispers low, *Thou must,*
   The youth replies, *I can.*

Ralph Waldo Emerson

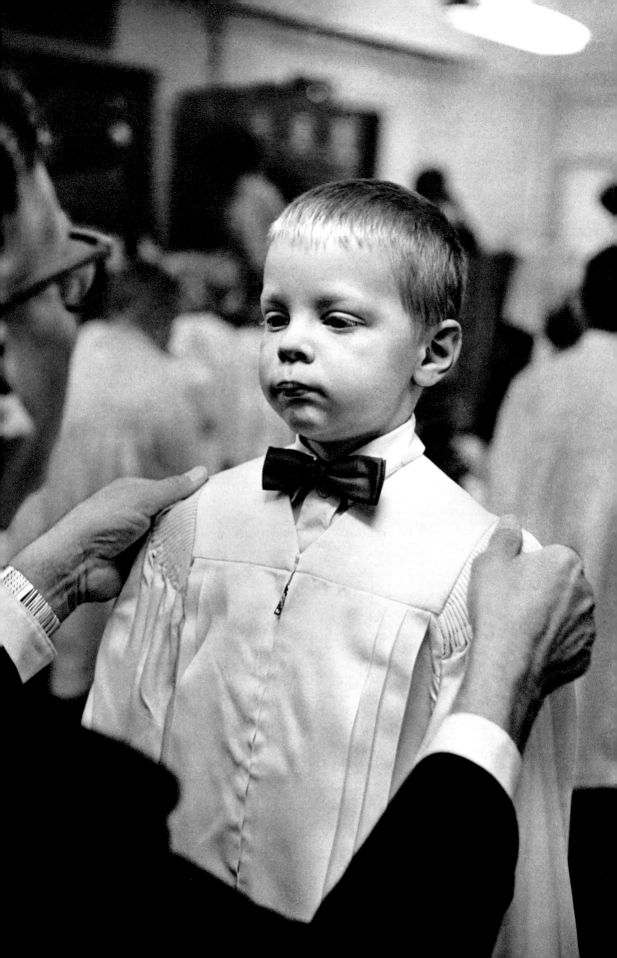

Her children rise up and call her blessed

I love these little people; and it is not a slight thing
when they, who are so fresh from God, love us.

Charles Dickens

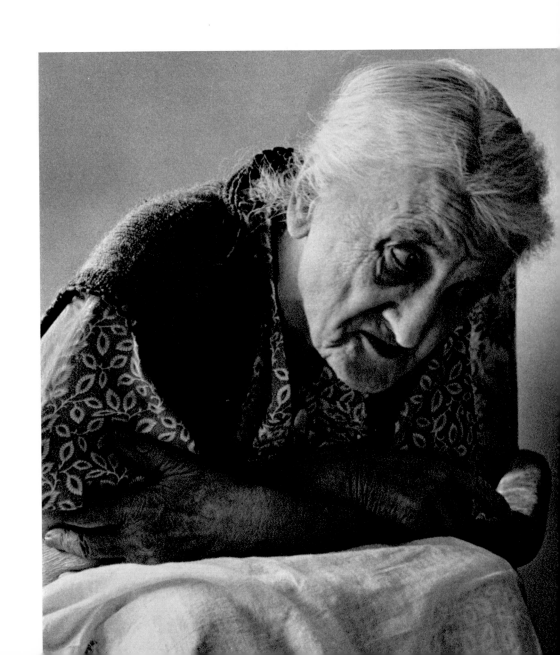

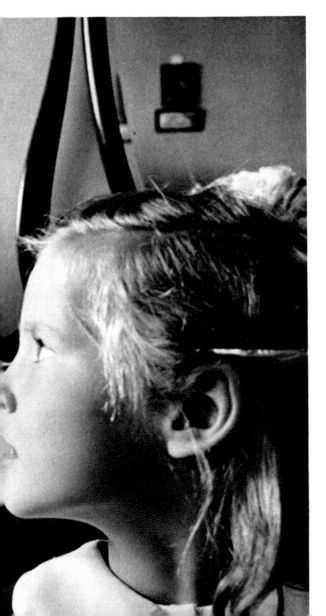

So much of what is great has sprung
from the closeness of family ties.

James Matthew Barrie

Children are principally the creatures of example—whatever surrounding adults do, they will do. If we strike them, they will strike each other. . . . If we habitually admit the right of sovereignty in each other and in them they will become equally respectful of our rights and of each other's.

Josiah Warren

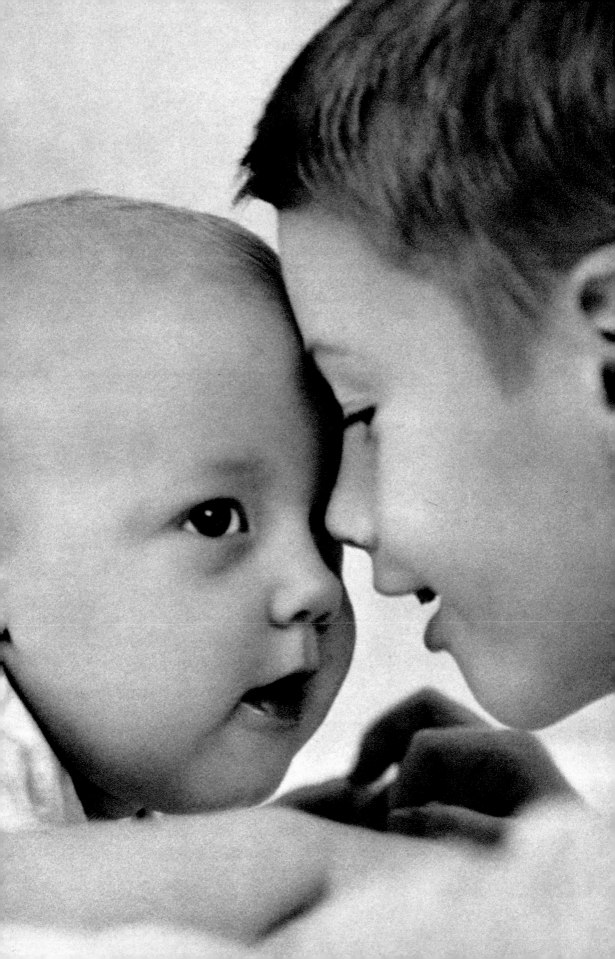

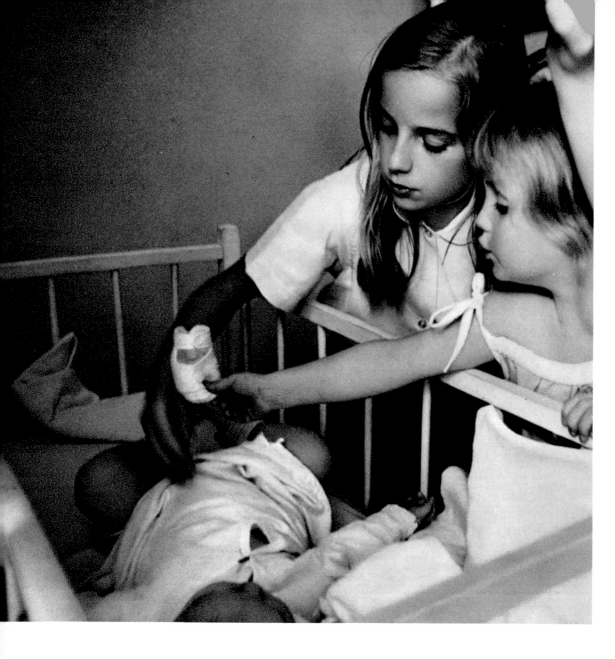

When I am the President
    Of these United States,
I'll eat up all the candy
    And swing on all the gates.

Anonymous

Why do the bells of Christmas ring?
Why do little children sing?
Once a lovely shining star,
Seen by shepherds from afar,
Gently moved until its light
Made a manger's cradle bright.

Eugene Field

A child's education
should begin at least
a hundred years
before he is born.

Oliver Wendell Holmes

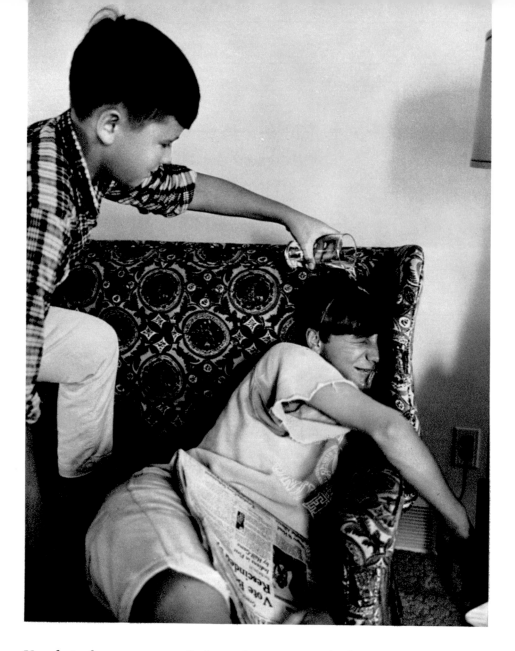

Youth is the time to go flashing from one end of the
world to the other both in mind and body; to try the manners of
different nations; to hear the chimes at midnight;
to see sunrise in town and country; to be converted at a revival;
to circumnavigate the metaphysics, write halting verses,
run a mile to see a fire.

Robert Louis Stevenson

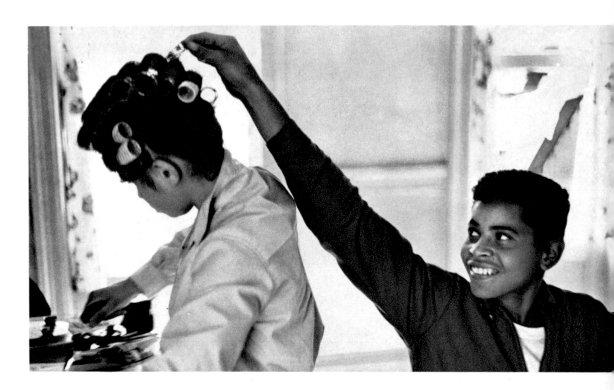

Youth, large, lusty, loving—youth full of grace, force, fascination, do you know that Old Age may come after you with equal grace, force, fascination?

Walt Whitman

We understand death for the
first time when he puts his
hand upon one whom we love.

Madame de Staël

51

As a white candle
In a holy place,
So is the beauty
Of an aged face.

Joseph Campbell

To make your children capable of honesty is the beginning of education.

John Ruskin

My heart is at rest within my breast,
And everything else is still.

William Blake

Good family life is never an accident
but always an achievement by those who share it.

James H.S. Bossard

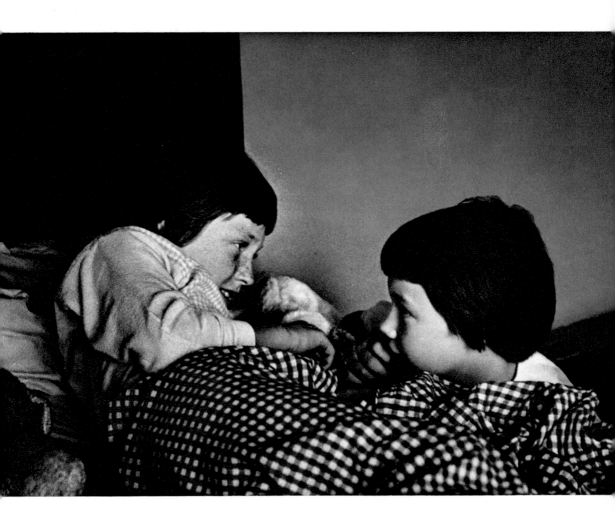

Be like the bird
That, pausing in her flight
Awhile on boughs too slight
  Feels them give way
Beneath her and yet sings,
Knowing that she hath wings.

Victor Hugo

Sweet childish days, that were as long as twenty days are now.

William Wordsworth

There is an enduring tenderness in the love of
a mother to a son that transcends all other
affections of the heart . . . she will glory in his
fame and exult in his prosperity; and, if
adversity overtake him, he will be the dearer
to her by misfortune.

Washington Irving

I was ever of the opinion, that the honest man who married and brought up a large family, did more service than he who continued single and only talked of population.

Oliver Goldsmith

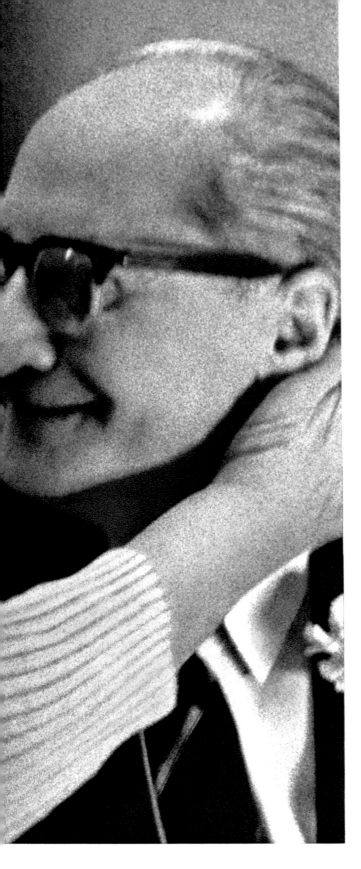

There is a peculiar beauty
about godly old age—the
beauty of holiness.
Husband and wife who have
fought the world side by
side, who have made common
stock of joy or sorrow,
and become aged together,
are not unfrequently found
curiously alike in personal
appearance, in pitch and
tone of voice, just as
twin pebbles on the beach,
exposed to the same tidal
influences, are each
other's alter ego.

Alexander Smith

What is the little one thinking about?
Very wonderful things, no doubt;
Unwritten history!
Unfathomed mystery!
Yet he laughs, and cries, and eats, and drinks.
And chuckles and crows, and laughs and winks,
As if his head were as full of kinks
And curious riddles as any Sphinx.

Josiah Gilbert Holland

God, what a world, if men in street and mart
Felt that same kinship of the human heart
Which makes them, in the face of fire and flood,
Rise to the meaning of True Brotherhood.

Ella Wheeler Wilcox

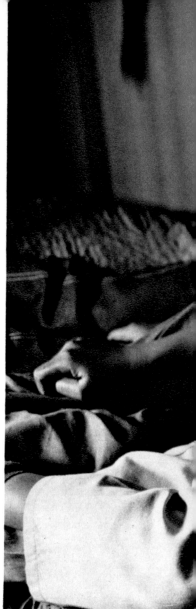

We ought to hear at least one little song every day, read a good poem, see a first-rate painting, and if possible speak a few sensible words.

Johann Wolfgang von Goethe

If a man does not keep pace with his companions, perhaps it is because he hears a different drummer. Let him step to the music he hears, however measured or far away.

Henry David Thoreau

The youth gets together his materials to build a bridge to
the moon, or, perchance, a palace or temple on the earth . . .

Henry David Thoreau

"I'm quite as big for me," said he,
"As you are big for you."

John Kendrick Bangs

A woman is as old as she looks to a man that likes to look at her.

Finley Peter Dunne

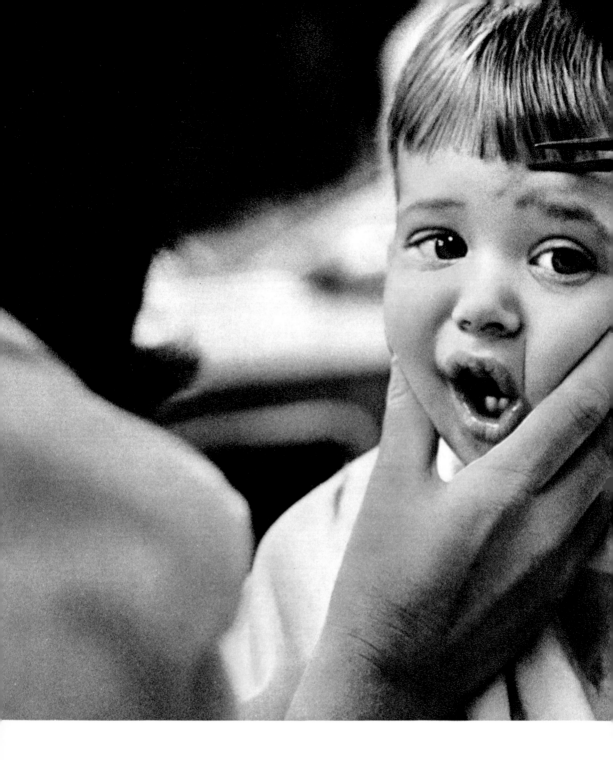

When children are taught not merely to know things but particularly to know themselves, not merely how to do things but particularly how to compel themselves to do things, they may be said to be really educated.

Edwin Grant Conklin

All the duties of religion are eminently solemn and venerable in the eyes of children. But none will so strongly prove the sincerity of the parents; none so powerfully awaken the reverence of the child ... as family devotions, particularly those in which petitions for the children occupy a distinguished place.

Timothy Dwight

A happy family is but an earlier heaven.

Sir John Bowring

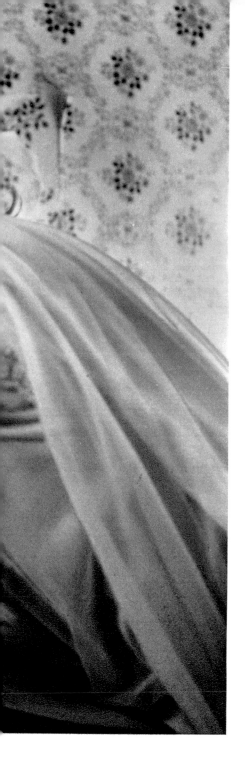

So for the mother's sake the child was dear,
And dearer was the mother for the child.

Samuel Taylor Coleridge

I still find each day too short for all the thoughts I want to think...

. . . all the walks I want
to take, all the books I want
to read and all the
friends I want to see.
The longer I live, the
more my mind dwells upon the
beauty and wonder of
the world.

John Burroughs

PHOTO CREDITS—Cover & frontispiece: George Daniell, Photo Researchers •
6-7: Christopher G. Knight, Photo Researchers • 8 top: Charles Harbutt,
Magnum • 8 bottom: Bruce Davidson, Magnum • 9: Elliott Erwitt,
Magnum • 11: Dwayne Bey, Bethel • 12: Dennis Stock, Magnum •
13: Costa Manos, Magnum • 14: Susan McCartney, Photo Researchers •
15: Grete Mannheim, Photo Researchers • 16: Doris Pinney, Photo-Library
• 17: Fritz Henle, Photo Researchers • 18 top: John Rees, Black Star •
18 bottom: Stephen Frisch, Photo Researchers • 19 top: John Rees,
Black Star • 19 bottom: Sergio Larrain, Magnum • 20 top: Erika,
Photo Researchers • 20 bottom: Bob Lerner, Look Magazine • 21:
Eve Arnold, Magnum • 22-23: Erika, Photo Researchers • 24: John Rees,
Black Star • 25 top: John Rees, Black Star • 25 bottom:
Larry B. Nicholson, Photo Researchers • 27: Fred Lyon, Rapho-Guillumette
• 29: Guy Gillette, Photo Researchers • 30-31: Hella Hammid,
Rapho-Guillumette • 32: Cornell Capa, Magnum • 33 top: Stern, from
Black Star • 33 bottom: Myron Wood, Photo Researchers • 34 top:
Bob Lerner, Look Magazine • 34 bottom: John Rees, Black Star • 35:
John Rees, Black Star • 37: Fred Lyon, Rapho-Guillumette • 38:
Matt Herron, Black Star • 39 top: Wayne Miller, Magnum • 39 bottom:
Robert S. Smith, Rapho-Guillumette • 40: Bruce Roberts,
Rapho-Guillumette • 41 top: Erika, Photo Researchers • 41 bottom:
Jackie Curtis, Photo Researchers • 43: Robert S. Smith, Rapho-Guillumette
• 44: Bruce Roberts, Rapho-Guillumette • 45 top: Grete Mannheim,
Photo Researchers • 45 bottom: Bruce Roberts, Rapho-Guillumette
• 46: Burk Uzzle, Magnum • 47: Eve Arnold, Magnum • 48:
Bruce Roberts, Rapho-Guillumette • 49: Charles Harbutt, Magnum •
50: Eve Arnold, Magnum • 53: William Stone, Photo Researchers
• 54: Elliott Erwitt, Magnum • 55: C. Robert Lee, Photo Researchers •
56: Sean Kernan, Bethel • 58-59: Elliott Erwitt, Magnum • 60 top:
Bruce Roberts, Rapho-Guillumette • 60 bottom: John Rees, Black Star •
61: Michael Sullivan, Black Star • 62 top: Grete Mannheim,
Photo Researchers • 62 bottom: John Russell • 63 top: Doris Pinney,
Photo-Library • 63 bottom: Esther Henderson, Rapho-Guillumette
• 64: Burk Uzzle, Magnum • 65: Bruce Roberts, Rapho-Guillumette •
66 top: Jane Latta, Photo Researchers • 66 bottom: Martha Reker,
Photo Researchers • 67: Erika, Photo Researchers • 68: Marion Bernstein,
Bethel • 71: Cornell Capa, Magnum • 72: Hella Hammid,
Rapho-Guillumette • 73: Archie Liberman, Look Magazine • 74:
Matt Herron, Black Star • 75: Fonssagrives, Photo Researchers •
76: Marc & Evelyne Bernheim, Rapho-Guillumette • 77: Ted Spiegel,
Bethel • 78: Joe Munroe, Photo Researchers • 79 top: J. W. Cella,
Photo Researchers • 79 bottom: Fritz Henle, Photo Researchers • 80:
Edward Lettau, Photo Researchers • 82-83: Frederick C. Baldwin,
Photo Researchers • 85: Doris Pinney, Photo-Library • 86-87:
Don Gettsug, Rapho-Guillumette • 88: John Rees, Black Star • 89:
Charles Harbutt, Magnum • 90: Dick Davis, Photo Researchers •
91: Laszlo Hege, Photo Researchers • 92: Marion Bernstein, Bethel
• Larry Silverstein, Photo Researchers

Printed and bound by Arnoldo Mondadori, Verona, Italy